C000097378

What Does Good Look Like?

Defining the Vision and Standards that Drive Better Habits and Results

(c) 2018 Smartspeed Consulting Limited. All rights reserved.

Disclaimer:

The author of this book has tried to present the most accurate information to his knowledge at the time of writing. This book is intended for information purposes only. The author does not imply any results to those using this book, nor are they responsible for any results brought about by the usage of the information contained herein.

No part of this book may be reprinted, electronically transmitted or reproduced in any format without the express written permission of the author.

Table of Contents

The Introduction

Welcome to **What Does Good Look Like?**

There is no great mystery about what I am going to share with you in this book; we're going to look at how we can articulate our operational visions and standards more effectively so that we get the results that we want for our business. This is often easier said than done and that is the point of this book. By the end of our time together I am expecting that you will find it much easier to share with your team what good looks like in a number of business areas. You will also have the tools and processes at your disposal to help you achieve your vision by systematically living and breathing the right behaviours. Every day you will be living your operational vision, if you apply the ideas from this book.

This book is aimed at managers and directors that want to achieve more from their business, want easier days and for their teams to be clearer about 'what good looks like' so that great results can follow. Too much time is wasted in business by not being crystal clear about what good actually looks like and so we end up hoping that common sense prevails and then getting angry when stupid things happen. This book is not about spoon feeding your staff, it is all about being effective at communicating what good looks like and getting real results.

If you are wondering how this book fits in with other books on the topic of vision think of the book you have in your hands as being a supporter of strategic visioning. The usual term 'vision' is directed at the big picture of where the business is going to and what it could become. In my experience this high-level vision is great for strategic planning but often poorly translated into an operational vision. That is where this book comes in. Depending on where your business is right now this book can help support the big picture vision in one of two main ways. Firstly, if you don't have a big picture vision you will at least end up with a picture of operational excellence that should push your business in the right direction from a results perspective (effectively a ground up approach to driving your business forward). Secondly, if you do have a big picture vision you should find yourself better able to articulate what the day to day operational side of your business needs to do, how it should behave and how it works so that your big picture is realised.

On its own 'what does good look like?' is a powerful question. You can get a long way just by asking that question.

This book will give you more than just this question, it will take you on a journey where we will look at several methods for helping to define what good looks like for your business. It is my expectation that one of these methods, or a combination of these methods, will provide your business with an effective approach for developing visions and setting standards.

Once we have this knowledge under our belt I will then take you through a short journey of determining an appropriate and effective action plan to help move your business in the right direction. A key chapter in this journey is 'The New Habits' which includes the idea of developing 'killer questions' to help drive the right behaviours throughout the activities and processes that make up the operational component of your business.

I have striven to make this book practical in nature. You will hopefully be able to read this book in a short period of time and be able to extract a number of useful strategies to help your business progress and develop rapidly and achieve the results that you want and need.

Before I jump into the first technique for articulating what good looks like, let me share with you some of the issues that surround not effectively describing to your colleagues a vision of excellence.

The Problems

The basic idea that I stated in the introduction probably doesn't seem like a big deal to most people - how bad can it get if you can't describe 'good'? The basic problem isn't usually a show stopper but let me expand a little on this to add a little more context to the purpose of this book.

Big pictures can be vague

When you are trying to paint a picture, a vision, for your business it can sometimes be easy to conjure up a description. OK, it might not be easy all the time, but to talk about where you want your business to get to and what you want it to become, can allow you to talk about vague ideas. It is unlikely that anyone will pick you up for this approach and it is what many businesses do.

I don't particularly have a problem with this approach if it can be easily translated into strategy and operational activity. If you need to develop your visions into something a little more concrete, then the ideas in this book will help you to develop something more definite and tangible for your teams.

Small pictures can be missed out

On the opposite end of the spectrum are the small pictures. These can include the standards we define for our housekeeping activities, the completion of standard tasks, the way meetings should be run and anything else you can think of that is routine and operational for your business.

Being articulate about these matters is easier than the big picture stuff for most of us. Let's be honest, there is less riding on the ability to define the correct way to measure an oil level in a machine than illuminate a pathway to the business' holy grail.

Standard Operating Procedures (SOPs), Key Performance Indicators (KPIs), objectives, 5S (a practical and effective organisation and efficiency methodology) all do a pretty fine job of helping us to agree on 'what good looks like' at the grass roots level. However, there are many other tasks, situations, behaviours and experiences that we don't apply the same logic to and this book will help you to get the most out of these situations also.

Middle pictures can be hard

So, if big pictures are often vague and little pictures often don't cover everything what does that do for our 'middle pictures'? By middle pictures I am referring to the bit of our business that links vision and strategy with the operational arms of our business. Or, in other words, how do we bend and shape our business processes so that we can achieve the objectives and vision that the business is destined for?

I find that this is often a neglected element in the business, the filling in the sandwich that binds the future of the business with the minutiae of the day-to-day. We spend so little time trying to get excited about this topic that it usually gets lost somewhere in the busy-ness of the working day and rarely pops up in conversation until one of the many 'wheels' fall off and a crisis occurs.

This book will certainly help you to focus on this part of the business dynamic. If correctly applied, you will end up with clearer visions, more effective processes and better habits at all levels of your hierarchy that more fully describe 'what good looks like' across the operational landscape of your organisation.

We put up with what good doesn't look like!

How many times have you walked past, or participated in, a situation in your business that you know is sub-optimal? I'll give you some examples from some of my clients (before we changed things, of course!):

- Meetings that take way too long, don't produce any meaningful actions and allow certain individuals to steer the meetings to suit their own agenda.
- Design processes that don't follow the prescribed rules of how the business needs to work and lead to expensive mistakes being consistently made.
- Investing time and energy to highlight deficiencies elsewhere in the business, rather than 'putting your own house in order' by taking an inwards look at what is going on and making each team responsible for looking after itself properly.
- Production environments that are untidy, unsafe and are not readily presentable to customers.
- Computer systems that have incomplete data in them and that cannot be used for management reporting in a meaningful way.
- Not having the right training for the business' in-house

software so that, instead of efficiently operating an administrative process, it limps on (with everyone involved being unhappy about the situation).

- Training being booked last minute and the individuals in the business that need to demonstrate their competency through formal courses scraping through at the last minute.
- Staff that aren't doing a good enough job not being told this, until a formal appraisal situation arises.
- Not having the right tools for a maintenance task and taking a really long (and noticeably long) time to complete a relatively simple task.
- Overloading the business with the wrong kind of work and rewarding those responsible whilst punishing the people who cannot deliver the promises.
- Not developing effective escalation routes and watching the business get stuck with the same issues over and over again.

I could carry on, but I am sure that you can nod your head to at least one or two of the items on this list. If we know what bad looks like then we have the opportunity to do something about it. We'll look at this in more detail later, but I want you to start thinking about what good looks like, or at least things that you don't like that you can come back to later.

Our day-to-day working doesn't move us toward our vision

It is also an issue for many businesses that, if we do have a picture of what good looks like, then our day to day actions and behaviours don't always align. We may pull ahead in a few areas of the business that help to achieve certain strategic objectives, but other areas could well be lacking.

If you are familiar with the Sales and Operations Planning (S&OP) approach that many businesses utilise you will recall the balancing activity that takes place. All primary functions of a business need to pull in the same direction and at the same time, with the same level of effort. Most S&OP processes attempt to rebalance the efforts in all of these main areas so that the business does move together in one direction at the same time; you can think of this being similar to coordinating a huge three-legged race (or, more likely, a seven-legged-race). If one of the runners moves too quickly and / or in the wrong direction the team stumbles and falls over. The same is for the S&OP process and it is also the same for the day-to-day operations resembling building blocks of the vision of the business.

This book will look at a number of strategies to help you refine how your days operate so that you do continuously move towards the vision for your business.

What if your big picture is 'limited'?

This topic is another interesting challenge for any business. What happens when you don't know if your picture is limited?

I have been in many conversations over the years where it became clear that the people I was working with weren't clear about what good did look like. As I write this section three examples jump to mind:

- A badly organised production environment, where the operatives worked inefficiently, wasn't seen as an issue because that's how they always did it!
- A sales team didn't think that knowing their win rate and having an up to date sales order book was important. This led to ineffective working, inefficient workarounds and an inability to optimise results, but they had never seen anything different.

- A scheduling team for a services business spent their whole-time expediting customer issues and micromanaging the services team. They had limited experience of what a scheduling team should do and reverted to fire-fighting and certainly weren't getting out of second gear. They didn't know that a better option existed.

I could go on. In this book we will look at some ideas to get around this issue, but even by taking a time out to follow along with the exercises in this book, you will be able to generate something far more effective for your business. Not knowing how every other business in the world carries out their activities will not stop you. Some experience of what good looks like is great, but not essential.

How do you lead your team to victory if the picture isn't clear?

This is another great point. If you cannot articulate where you want to take your business to (or a single function of your business, or even just your team) how effective do you think your journey will be?

I speak to lots of managers who 'kinda, sorta' know where they need to take their team to (and what kinds of behaviours and results look good), but never get around to properly describing them. So, any results they get look OK to their teams, leading to the manager becoming highly frustrated!

This book will help to get you past this issue and will enable the team to be able to get behind the vision that has been defined, with clear direction in terms of what they need to do in order to achieve that vision.

As a case in point, I have recently been working with a team (well, a collection of individuals that loosely call themselves a team) that weren't producing the results they needed to. We sensitively explored the issues at hand and discussed how a great team works together to help each other to achieve their goals. Within minutes we had a description of how a good team works together and fleshed out a number of 'what does good look like' examples that we could use as guides going forward.

Not everything stuck, but enough of their mini-visions of excellence did stick that their performance notably changed in a very short period of time. As you progress through this book it is my aim that you will be able to do the same and lead your team to victory.

This book offers options

What I want to achieve with this book is to give you some options to help you generate more effective visions for your business and then give you some practical options as to how you can put them into effect.

My approach might seem a little mechanical and process focused, I am an engineer by profession, so you will have to indulge me a little bit in this area. What I want to do is let you have access to is some ideas that you can then bend, twist and bash into a shape that suits the needs of your business.

I have structured this book so that it fundamentally comes in two halves. If you need to direct your focus to only the execution of your strategy, then you can jump straight to part two. If you want some ideas to better define the vision of what good looks like for your business, then you can simply carry on.

I feel that you will get the most value from this book if you read it from start to finish, to get a good measure of the options and ideas I am sharing with you and then make a decision as to how this material can best be fitted to your business.

I have intentionally kept the book brief as I actually do want people to be able to read and absorb the material and then put the bits that make sense to them into practice. Most of us are strapped for time (or at least feel this way) and I don't want to burden you any further.

Objectives

What do you want to achieve from this book?

Do you have a list of objectives that you need to achieve, either for your own personal gain or for your business?

You will get more out of this book if you have some objectives in mind and I encourage you to have a think about this now. You might also be thinking "what could I achieve from this book?". If that is the case, here are some objectives that my clients have had in the past when I have used the approaches I am going to share with you in the pages to follow:

- Moving out of 'Groundhog Day' and towards realising the planned strategy.

- Stopping the stupid mistakes that happen on a 'all too regular' basis.

- Achieving a level of performance that matches the ideals held in the heads of the people in charge of the business.

- Slicker, faster and more effective processes.

- Identifying improvements that can make a tangible and lasting change to the profitability of the business.

- The desire to get promoted from delivering results for a line manager / director.

Your objectives may well fall into one of the above examples or be a combination of them. Whatever you need to achieve (and the last one is a true example which did result in a promotion, by the way) please make sure that you have a good idea of 'what good looks like' for you.

Recommended approach

So, how do I think that you'll get the most out of this book?

I recommend that you read through the book once yourself (it shouldn't take too long) and decide which of the tools you think will be most appropriate for both your own personal style for making change happen and the needs of your business. Then I would ask that you consider pulling a small team together. You might want to do some thinking on your own, but when you are ready to start sharing your ideas you'll most likely need a team around you to help form and further shape the ideas so that you can start to implement them.

The team that I am suggesting doesn't have to be your own team, it could be a cross section of staff that you know to have useful skills at making improvements a reality and ideally have a similar view of the world to yourself.

The action plan that you will create on the back of this book should become your blueprint for a more effective business, so I guess it is time to move from the Introduction and into Part 1.

Are you ready to get started?

Part 1

Approaches to generate a vision of 'what good looks like'

The Four Approaches

In this section of the book I want to share with you four approaches that can help you to paint a better picture of what good looks like for your business. The approaches themselves can be used in isolation or, ideally, stacked on top of each other. In fact, there is a large overlap between the different approaches, but their differences are enough that I felt it was worthwhile to treat them as such.

The four approaches are:

The Gap – Spotting the elements of your business that are missing and describing what that gap is.

The Flip – Taking the frustrations from the working day and creatively inverting them to define a better place to operate from.

The Copy – Using the experience and ideas of other organisations to boost your own vision of excellence.

The Breakdown – Articulating what good looks like through a small steps approach.

As you have probably gathered from what I have written so far, I am not offering you a prescription to create visions for your business. I am offering you some practical options and some ideas on how to make sure the change manifests and sticks. You may wish to play with the approaches and see what happens and then combine the other approaches as you see fit. You can also add in your own methods to the mix as you develop your approach, or you can put it all into the plan from day one. Control and choice in this matter is in your hands.

I am bothered about you achieving significant and tangible results; I want you to focus on what you want to achieve rather than how you will get there at this moment in time. So, let me move into the first approach and let's get this show on the road!

The Gap

As I mentioned in the last section, the gap approach is simply a way of spotting what isn't present in your business. It is quick to apply, and you probably have a good list of issues already.

You are here!

What doesn't work in your business?

What loose ends do you have?

What recurring problems do you face?

The answers to these three questions will shed a light on where some of the gaps are present in your business. The reactive tasks that crop up, that derail your day, are the area of focus for this approach to help you draw out elements for your vision. Being realistic about your shortcomings, about the areas of your business that haven't been thought through or formalised, is a great place to start. Make a list of these items.

What results do you need?

What results are you missing?

What performance levels haven't you achieved that you really need to?

What objectives haven't been completed?

This is another way of looking at the gaps in your business. The first set of questions was about the processes, this set is about the results. Considering the results that you want to / are required to achieve is another great way to focus on what gaps are in your business.

If you are part of a line management structure you will most likely be acutely aware of what performance levels you are not achieving. Make a list of any of the results gaps that you can think of.

Scores out of ten

Look at the departments that are present in your business. What is their purpose? Can you define it?

For each of those departments allocate a score out of ten. Ten would represent that the department is living and breathing their purpose. Zero would represent that they are as far away as possible as you can get from being 'on purpose'.

Any number less than ten is a gap, you can add this to your list of gaps as you build the picture of where you have work to do. This scoring approach is a little subjective, but it is a great way to start a conversation, if handled in the right way. If you can support your scoring with evidence, then you can have an easier discussion with your colleagues when the time comes.

Let me give you a quick example of a department and their purpose. Considering a purchasing function. You could describe their activities in a number of ways, but a simple description could be:

To source and procure products for the business in a cost effective manner from partnership orientated suppliers that deliver on time (all the time), to our required schedules of activity.

Instantly you have a feel for what a 'ten' looks like.

Defining the width of the gap

Pull the three lists you have from previous activities together (missing items, results unobtained and departments not living 'on purpose') into one document. This next step is going to help you determine a weighting for each of those gap items (and you can use this approach with the other visioning methods too).

For each item I would like you to score it against these three factors, to create a score / weighting:

Benefit

If the benefit of closing out the gap is really significant for your business, give it a high score out of ten.

If, on the other hand, the closing of this gap will make little impact for the business, give it a low score out of ten.

Cost

Like the previous factor score this one out of ten also.

A low cost / relatively free cost for closing out the gap will give you a high score out of ten, whilst an expensive / resource draining cost will give you a low score out of ten.

Speed

A rapid closing out of the gap (such as today / tomorrow) will yield a high score in this area and a long and drawn out affair (several months and the need to go through various committees) will give this factor a low score out of ten.

To calculate your total score (the BCS score as I call it), multiply the scores you have given each gap for each factor together. This should give you a score between 1 and 1000. Once you have the scores calculated for each gap you should then be able to rank them, and this should be your priority sequence as you head into the implementation stage.

To make sure that I have gotten this point across let me give you a quick example from my recent work history:

Option 1 – Introduce kitting to the production environment
Benefit = 10 / 10
Cost = 6 / 10
Speed = 4 / 10
BCS = 10 x 6 x 4 = 240

Option 2 – Improve the flow of data to the production teams
Benefit = 8 / 10
Cost = 9 / 10
Speed = 8 / 10

BCS = 8 x 9 x 8 = 576

If I went off gut feel alone I would have ventured down the kitting (option 1) path. However, from doing the simple maths it becomes clear to me that I need to focus on the data issue first. On reflection this makes sense as I can have a big jump in performance now, and then work on the kitting issue when I have some of the other obstacles that are slowing down that potential implementation out of the way.

Forming the vision

Now that you have a prioritised list of gaps in your business, you can start to use this document to help share your vision with your team. As I said earlier in this book, the next three vision developing strategies are designed to slot together or be used independently. I recommend that you keep this list on standby and augment it by using the additional methods I am going to share with you in this part of the book.

In this section we have looked at the gaps in the business, in the next section we will look at inverting poor performance and hopefully you will be able to add some more detail to your vision of what good looks like for your business.

Recap

- Identify gaps for:
    - missing items
    - results unobtained
    - departments not living 'on purpose'

Score the remedy of each gap using the BCS scoring method and prioritise the results.

The Flip

This next method is another simple approach that is a good way to engage your teams with both continuous improvement and helping to develop a vision for the future. This method can help with a bottom up view of what needs to change in a business and rarely scares people (as it often does when you say that you going to undertake a visioning exercise!).

What don't you want?

One of the easiest conversations to get into with staff members is a 'whinge' about what isn't working in the business. Show me any business and I'll quickly find someone that likes to 'tell it how it is' and tell me all about the things that don't work properly. You'll know who these people are in your own business and that isn't the challenge.

The challenge is to sort the 'wheat from the chaff' and coax your team to provide you with some solutions for the real issues in the business. Be careful not to dismiss genuine issues that are being faced by the business but, like the BCS scoring in the last chapter, not all issues are equal. The flip method can help your team to move past the stuck phase (where they don't know a solution, just issues) into creating a vision that can help you to generate a meaningful set of actions to move you towards a better result.

What "X" said

X is the person that is stuck in your business. They are stuck in my clients' business too. They used to be stuck when they worked for me too, until I found some ways to help them get unstuck.

What does X say in your business? Let me give you some examples from the last couple of years that have stuck in my mind:

- The MRP system is giving me stupid orders to place.
- Our meetings take too long and don't do anything useful.
- The maintenance team don't start work when they should.
- The manager in charge is incompetent.
- Our strategy doesn't work.
- We keep on making the same mistakes, over and over again.
- There's nothing written down.
- My colleague doesn't know what they are doing!

- It is quicker for me to do it than to teach someone else how to do it.
- It's complicated and that is why mistakes are being made.
- You can't put it into a process – it's a 'black art'.

And I am sure that as you read this brief list you are now rhyming off other issues (and excuses) that are thrown your way on a daily basis. OK, let's do something with these issues.

Inversion

The simplest thing you can do with your list of grumbles is to invert them. Flip them upside down and try to turn a negative into a positive.

A conversation I had very recently with someone (referred to as 'X' below) that was grumbling was at a client's office. The conversation went a little something like this:

GJ – "Can we have a chat about the schedule for your service team?"

X – "We can, but the information is garbage!"

GJ – "What do you mean, exactly?"

X – "The automatic scheduler keeps on giving out rubbish information, it takes an age to review it and make sense out of it which then stops me from doing my other work."

GJ – "So, what happens?"

X – "So I don't bother looking at it at all."

GJ - "What is the result of not looking at the scheduler?"

X – "We end up missing slots in the plan and having to fire-fight. That's what we spend most of our time doing."

GJ – "Can we fix the scheduler?"

X – "I don't know."

GJ – "Do you want a different day-to-day experience of working with your scheduling tool?"

X – "Definitely!"

GJ – "What would you want?"

X – "I want to be able to look at the scheduler and within a couple of minutes know exactly what I need to do so that I can get on with the rest of my tasks and know that I have taken care properly of the service teams."

Aha… That seems like a pretty clear vision of what good looks like, but it can take a little coaxing from your team members to get it out of them. Inverting issues, 'the flip', is a great way to do this.

The above example is pretty much word for word from a case the other week. X, in this case, was resigned to poor systems and working patterns. The reality was, in this case, that X was causing their own system problems. Having the vision was essential to getting buy in to solve the issue; fixing the issue might well be a different story. We will come to the solution and implementation work in the next section of this book, for the time being let's keep focused on how to generate effective visions for what good looks like for our business.

Inversion and upgrade

Taking the idea of inverting problems a little further, when you tip an issue upside down what else can you do with it? This is an opportunity – for you to take an issue you have, trying to determine the opposite and then embellishing it into something really interesting and useful.

In the last example the conversation got us to a point where the scheduling tool could be trusted and it would only take a few minutes to process the information. 'Pretty good' I hear you say, but could there be something better than this? If you start to think about this situation, what could you add to the solution to make it an even better outcome?

This book is called 'What Does Good Look Like?' and you could arguably agree that this solution does look good. Let us, for the time being, suspend the word good and replace it with amazing. What does amazing look like, in this situation?

Could the scheduling tool be automated? Could it be deskilled and passed on to another member of staff (allowing X to use their talents to greater effect)? Could we come up with a way to eliminate the need for scheduling in the first place? Could we speed up the delivery process so that another outcome could be achieved?

So many possibilities... As a side note, I have been involved with scheduling systems where their elimination was possible (which had been a 45+ hours per week job at one point) and another case comes to mind where full automation was possible (saving over 80 hours per months from a time strapped team). Inversion is a great tool but inverting and upgrading of issues can really deliver some interesting opportunities when it comes to using problems to drive the creation of a vision for your business.

Drawing out a list

Pull together the inverted issues and start to build a vision for what good looks like. Remember, you can use all of the methods in this section to gain different perspectives in order to create a fuller and more explicit vision for your business.

The inversion method is a great place to start when you are trying to create your view of the future because the pain of today is real and tangible to your team. The idea of killing their specific issues can allow you to gain quick traction with changing the way the business works. This traction can allow you to quickly gain momentum and take on other challenges that you might planned for, that take you past just fixing broken parts of your business.

So, list out all of your inverted (and upgraded) problems and let's move to the next option for generating a vision for what good looks like for your business.

Recap

- List out what you no longer want to experience in your business.
- Flip these experiences into something that you do want

to experience.

- Review what you have written down and see if you can upgrade the inverted issues further, into something really amazing.

The Copy

'The Copy' is a great technique to use when you haven't had much past experience of what good looks like. Being in a stable period of employment is a nice feature of a career to many people, but a lack of exposure of different ways of working doesn't necessarily lead to the best ways of working. In many ways this cross fertilisation of ideas is a little like the evolution vs. inbreeding argument, but there is a way to get out of this situation.

Who is great at doing this already?

Are there any companies in your industry that are known to be good at what you do? Can you find out what they do differently to you and get some ideas from this review? There are many trade journals that can give you insights into what the best are doing and case studies in books that tell you about their approaches. Visits are often arranged by industry groups too that can help you to gain access to witness different ways of working. All of these options can help you to see what the best in your industry are up to and can provide you with lots of ideas on what good could look like.

But, here is a challenge for you, what if your particular industry is stuck in a rut and the best in your sector is only a few percentage points ahead of where you are performance wise? What do you do in this situation? What could good look like, I mean really look like? In this situation you might need to look outside of your industry.

Outside of your industry

What do other industries do that you could borrow, or bend, to suit the challenges and aspirations of your business?

I used to work in the power generation sector and everyone in that 'game' used to be the same – dusty, old and uninspired. A few of the automotive principles I had learned at another employer allowed us to completely reinvent ourselves and become one of the top performers globally.

One of my clients took this idea and changed one of their service departments based on the wisdom of a large coffee chain. The coffee chain's approach to customer service and processing people through a sequential series of steps paralleled their world and allowed for a number of insights to be gained. They used these insights to quadruple the productivity of one of their teams.

Another client was trying to figure out how to speed up their business processes and specifically the handover between departments. A chance conversation with a member of staff that was serious about their athletic training and how a relay race operates immediately provided food for thought. The description of a slick handover was described by their team and the key principles were then applied to the business' activities. They dropped the time it took to process their information packs down from weeks to hours.

If a pre-flight checklist is good enough for a pilot then it is surely good enough for the start of day routine for a doctor's practice. When a doctors' practice applied this idea to their working days their performance significantly improved. There were no longer preparation issues, there were no longer delays in processing paperwork, there were no longer people waiting to get their prescriptions at the counter; their productivity soared. Many of the small niggles of the day were ironed out because they borrowed ideas from other places / situations and industries.

Can you do the same? Can you look anywhere other than your colleagues and your competitors to find inspiration. I think that the answer is 'yes', but I leave this up to you to find out for yourself!

Look for the principles

What the other business or industry does is less important than the principle behind the activity. In some cases the application will be identical and you can transfer it straight into your business. In other cases you might need to spot the underlying principle and then translate the idea into your business. Looking again at the examples in the last section, let us look at the underlying principles.

In the power generation company the automotive principles I referred to were literally that, not the methodologies. We adopted a 'single piece flow' approach (where minimum batch size was eliminated and the bumps in production were taken out). We also took the idea of harmonised business units to help with the coordination of internal supply between functions.

The learning points from the coffee chain's service approach led to a few principles for my client. These included using a line balance to ensure that the work was split evenly between the people serving, having the workspace set up so all of the information / tools were immediately available and to smile whilst you worked.

The principles taken from the relay race included practicing until you got good at handing over between functions, defining what good looked like during a handover (prepared, complete, appropriate and fast) and ensuring that all the parties involved agreed on the rules of the handover.

The pre-flight checklists we based on the principle that once you have started an activity it is either too risky or too expensive to start over again and therefore checking properly before you do start is a really good idea.

The principles may be obvious to you, or you might need to think it through. As I said before, if what someone is doing in another organisation doesn't look like it is directly reproducible in your business then try to look 'under the skin' and find the purpose of the activity / its principle and see if you can apply that to your business. Every methodology that you can read about, or can witness for yourself, has principles sitting behind them. Spot these and you can apply the essence of the idea quickly and easily to your business.

Twist bend and flex

Now that you have some 'new' principles to apply to your business the next challenge is to bend and flex them so that they can become meaningful for your business. The principle itself should make sense, however it may need to be refined by the context of your business. Let me give you an example.

The idea of pull production systems work on a very simple principle: you only 'produce' when the next step in the process requires more.

In a fast food restaurant, burgers only get produced once the levels of finished product drop below a certain level during peak hours (they are usually made to order outside of peak times).

In a fabrication plant, new products are only produced once other products have passed a bottleneck process.

In a doctors' surgery, patients are only examined when they are ill.

In a continuous improvement programme new projects are

only evaluated and embarked upon once an existing project is completed and capacity is available.

These are all the same basic principle, but the application is bent and twisted to ensure it fits the business challenge in question. This is your challenge – take the principles you have borrowed from other industries and bend and twist the application into a working solution for your business.

Your version, but better

Now that you have a number of alternative views on what good looks like for other organisations and industries you can compile them into a vision for your business. If you have already built up a view of what gaps you have in your business and what issues you would like to flip, then you can add these new items to that mix and start to build a more comprehensive vision for your business.

Reviewing your business in this manner allows you to stand on the shoulders of others. It is very likely that their experiences, challenges and successes are embodied in the methods you have witnessed elsewhere. If you can figure out how to apply these ideas / principles into your business then you can effectively shortcut the years it has taken another organisation to achieve their success. Deciding on what good looks like doesn't automatically sentence you to a long period of hard work!

In the next section we'll look at the last method for developing visions that I will share with you in this book – the simple idea of articulating small chunks of your business!

Recap

- Find competitors in your sector that are doing great things and list out what it is that they are doing that makes them great.

- Look outside of your sector for other businesses that are doing some great things, that you can borrow and list out what it is that they do exceptionally and how they appear to be doing it.

- Boil down all the good things that you have seen into their fundamental principles.

- Twist these principles so that you can find a way to apply them to your business.

- Decide on what good looks like if you copy the best ideas you can find.

The Breakdown

Let me quickly recap on what we have covered, to put this method into perspective. We have looked at identifying the gaps in the processes of our business, flipped current issues and borrowed great ideas and principles from the organisations that exist around us. This fourth, and final, method is all about articulation – ensuring that we fully express our vision by getting into the 'nitty gritty'.

One vision can be hard

I use this fourth method with my clients a lot, namely because asking someone to come up with an operational vision in their business can be a big ask. This very question often invokes the 'fight, flight or freeze' phenomenon and you end up with nothing useful. I'll touch briefly on a consideration around this precise issue in the next chapter, but for now I want you to feel comfortable that this method will allow you to get past any 'stuck' feeling you have had around the topic of creating visions.

There is another question that could be asked here. Is one vision statement for the entire business helpful? Follow the guidance in this chapter and then we can pick up this question in the next chapter.

Segment your business

To get your vision development process moving with this method I am going to invite you to chop it up into a number of smaller pieces. The size of the pieces is up to you and will depend on how your business is structured. Let me share with you how I would split up a business for this purpose and then you can modify it to suit your own needs:

- I would take a high-level process map and chunk it down into segments based on the physical flow of the process, or by the teams that it passes through.
- Each step in the process would become a sub-heading.
- The general tasks (that support the overall process) would then be listed / brainstormed and added as further sub-headings.

It's not a particularly complicated approach, but the result to bear in mind is that you want to break down your business into a whole lot of small chunks, which when combined with the 5W1H method will make a whole load of sense.

5W1H

5W1H stands for:

What

Where

When

Who

Why

How

(Five words beginning with W and one with H!)

These headings in their own right can help you to become more explicit with each segment, prompting you to describe what good looks like for each of these words.

Let me give you an example from a recent discussion I have had about streamlining a routine business meeting. The notes in brackets refer to today's reality if is different from the vision.

What – The daily production meeting.

Where – In the production office.

When – 10am each weekday morning.

Who – All prepared production team office staff (all production team office staff, often unprepared!).

Why – To ensure all of our business processes are on track (to look at the full order book – yes, everything!).

How – Monitor exceptions for all main process steps (review every line of the full order book, painfully!).

When I first discussed these issues with the team, in pretty much the same way I have listed the points above, they weren't sure if there was much of a change. The last two points however are different enough that the end result will be significantly different. The current method of working takes a long time, allows people to come to the meeting unprepared and looks only at problems that need to be remedied there and then (there is no consideration of preventing tomorrow's problems). The proposed way forward means that a little bit of preparation from each team member, with regards to any process breakdowns and what the remedy is, has the potential to speed up the meeting itself and head off issues before they start to hurt the business.

5W1H is a powerful and simple set of prompts that I hope you can use outside of this particular methodology, but for articulating the vision for a small segment of your business it is great. It might take little bit of practice to become explicit with your descriptions, but it will be well worth it.

Articulate each segment

For each segment you have identified for your business answer the questions of who, what, where, when, how and why and see what you can create. The process of writing this information down may well provoke your mind to answer the question of 'what does good look like' for each segment of your business.

Answering these questions can help to improve ownership of specific activities (who), improve the way an activity is carried out (how), reinforce the rationale and purpose of an activity (why), help to define business routines (when), confirm any location specific issues (where) and the specificity of the action itself (what). 5W1H is a basic business analysis tool, but its effectiveness makes it a heavyweight in anyone's improvement toolkit.

I used this approach to great effect with one of my clients. Their business was in a state of flux during a period of growth and needed a better definition of what good looked like. The following is the list of pointers made with their team as we started the journey to having an organisation that looked great from a perspective of effective stock management, efficient kitting and supportive planning operations:

Goods Inward

• Items are booked into the system within 1 hour of receipt.

• The Quality Control queue is the bible for goods inward inspection.

• Goods Inward is clear every evening.

• Only Goods Inward staff sign for deliveries and they are responsible for goods until booked in.

Stores

• All locations / bins are defined.

• Bar codes are present on all of the racking.

• The tablet / scanners are adopted and embraced by all Stores staff.

• Accuracy is 98% plus at all times.

• Perpetual inventory is in place.

• Disciplines are established and maintained.

• Stores staff 'own' inventory accuracy.

• Stores Key Performance Indicators (KPIs) are daily management tools (including stock accuracy, pick accuracy and pick speed).

• Floor space to be kept clear at all times.

• Good housekeeping is maintained.

Picking

• Locations have been optimised, along with the paperwork.

• Picking is swift and accurate.

• If items are not picked from the default location, or default is out of stock, appropriate transactions are undertaken.

Sales Orders (SO)

• The sales order book is our master schedule, which is visible across all departments, so everyone is working from the same information.

• Contract review for new orders is quick and effective, driven by system data.

• Forecasts are updated regularly by the planners.

Works Orders (WO)

• Works orders are Enterprise Resouce Planning (ERP) driven and updated daily.

• The works order accuracy allows the shop floor 'work to lists' to operate.

• The replenishment settings are refined for all manufacturing levels, allowing the works order book to replicate our planning approach.

• Capacity planning is accurate, trusted and relied upon.

Production cycle times are continuously refined against KPIs and actual production information.

Purchase Orders (PO)

•   The purchase order suggestions are ERP driven.

•   Last minute panics (for more stock) are few and far between.

•   Replenishment settings have been configured for all parts and the PO suggestions are valid over 99% of the time.

•   ERP suggestions are enacted each day.

•   A 'critical list' for manual override is maintained.

Shop Floor Data Capture

•   Operation information / bookings are captured in real time.

•   All operators are confident inputting into the system.

•   The work to list is Production's bible.

Engineering

•   Bills of Material and routes are accurate at all times.

•   Engineering development work is as disciplined as production in terms of Sales Order / Works Order / Purchase Order.

•   Engineering Change Notes (ECNs) cascade quickly and

effectively through the whole business, with a clear final sign off visible.

• ECNs are to be owned by the creator and it is his/her responsibly to ensure close out.

• ERP system to issue reminders to the creator when an ECN has not closed within the specified time period.

Spares

• Spare part requests flow through the business via the same contract review process that the Sales Order take.

• Confusion and stock issues are reduced to zero.

• Old revisions to be clearly labelled in both the Stores and on the ERP system.

General

• Routines and habits are defined (and matched with the Quality Management System) within the business that support the effective use of ERP.

• Clear responsibilities for all parts of the system are defined, published and measured.

• Key Performance Indicators that relate to the performance of ERP are agreed and used at management meetings to ensure system reliability.

• Key outputs from these habits are tied into routine

business meetings, making them visible and embedded.

• Housekeeping activities (for ERP) are defined and built into the routines to help maintain clean data at all times.

• Knowledge is captured (Standard Operating Procedures / skill matrices) and shared (toolbox talks) on an ongoing basis.

• Reports are developed and trusted.

• ERP runs on automatic wherever possible.

• Stock adjustments are identified, reported, approved and processed in both the ERP system and accounting software on a weekly basis.

I have given you the whole list as I have found that most businesses have fairly generic needs and that you might find items on the list above that you can consider when pulling your list together. The example doesn't precisely follow the 5W1H list of prompts as it was created in conjunction with a separate business routine document (when) and an organisation chart (who).

Link the chain together

Pull all of the 5W1H articulations that you have created and voila, you have another approach to creating a vision for your business. Ensure that you looked at each area of your business and defined what good looks like for each area.

Review this vision for completeness, to ensure that you haven't missed out any obvious areas from your business, and once done you should now have an explicit vision for operational performance in your business that can help drive the results that want you to see.

In the next chapter we will look at how we pull these four visioning methods together and choose the best way to articulate what does good look like for your business' operations.

Recap

- Breakdown your business into its major process steps.
- Use the 5W1H approach on each step to articulate what good looks like.
- Compile all of these smaller visions into one document.

Picking Your Vision Strategy

The ideas that I have shared in the last four chapters can be used either on their own, or in a combination of your choice. I believe that most businesses can get the most out of these approaches when they use a number in combination, let me expand upon this.

Methods

If you applied all four methods in a series, you might end up with an approach that looks a little like this:

- Perform a gap analysis of the functions that you are missing in your business.
- Flip the current mistakes and annoyances to produce a second list.
- Look outside of your organisation for ideas and directly transferrable solutions that you can apply to your business.
- Use the 5W1H approach to expand and articulate 'what good looks like' for each of the areas within your business, including the observations made from the previous three methods, to pull your list together.
- Voila, you have an operational vision that should close

out most (if not all) of the performance gaps you currently have and potentially allow you to transform the operational performance of your business.

Of course, you may choose to start small and use just 'the flip' and 'the breakdown' approaches to change some current issues by turning them into strengths. There is no right and wrong way to approach this; try out a few of these methods and see how you feel about them. Stacking them gives you better results, but if in doubt – start small and grow from there.

Applying the vision tools to different levels

The tools that I have shared in the past few pages can be applied in different ways, to different levels within your business, for different purposes. I will expand on this in just a moment.

The way that you tackle a business wide operational vision is usually different to that of a team or an individual in that way that you consider the width and depth of the descriptions you develop. A business wide operational vision may well be broad, but not generate too much detail (or depth). An operational vision for an individual (that perhaps is new or struggling) may well be narrow but very detailed (or, deep).

Again, you can layer these approaches to suit the needs of your business and ensure that 'what good looks like' cascades its way effectively through your organisation.

Business

As I said at the start of this book, the operational visions that you will create by following the advice in any of the last four chapters should help you to achieve your overall business vision (the big picture of where the business is going to). At this point it is a really good opportunity to make sure that the vision you have created for your business' operations aligns with the overall big picture. If it doesn't, review the two visions and make a decision on what you need to change.

From an operational vision point of view, you can apply these tools to the business in its entirety. From the sales and marketing side of the business, to the invoicing and customer care activities you can use these visioning tools to help you paint a picture of how your business could / should work and perform. Having a wide vision of performance can be a really useful framework to hang your continuous improvement projects from and as a baseline for future decision-making activities.

Departments and functions

One of the most effective ways that I have used operational visions is at the departmental, or functional, level. Breaking down the processes into their steps and ensuring that 'what good looks like' is described for each step is a great approach both for clarification of standards required and for designing how your processes should work and behave. When you spell out what good looks like and you share this with your team it means that they have received some reinforcement over the performance standards they are meant to adhere to. If the articulation you create isn't a current reality and can only be reached through changing how your business / team operates then you have a continuous improvement opportunity to focus your team on. When improvement projects can be linked back to making an individual's life easier, achieving strategic objectives of the business, or another noble cause, managing change projects becomes a lot easier and meaningful.

The example I gave in an earlier section was at the function level, although we covered so many areas in the order fulfilment process that it did in fact cover a great deal of the business. When you have an operational vision at the function level you can have grown up conversations with your team and your colleagues about how far away you are from achieving the vision. If you all agree and buy into the vision then you can keep each other accountable, with no one playing the villain in this story. The best bit, for me, is that it is usually only one or two little tweaks that need to be put into action in order to witness some tangible (and hopefully impressive) results. A little bit of clarification on what good looks like can go a long way.

Individuals

The third level of application I want to explore is the individual level. I should say here that this particular approach can say just as much about the manager as it does the individual, so it can serve as a double whammy.

For the individual it allows the manager to articulate the performance standards, routines, behaviours and expectations to the individual in question. There may be performance issues that have been identified, or repeating issues that are linked to the lack of activity in certain areas. Being clear with an individual makes supporting them a lot easier if they are crystal clear about what good looks like.

For the manager this is an opportunity to properly package and share with your team what you expect, need and want to experience. I have sat in far too many meetings where the wants of a manager haven't been clear to their team and a major source of their frustrations (on both parts). As I write this I recall a Managing Director complain bitterly that his Sales Director wasn't making enough visits to their key accounts. The Sales Director thought one visit a month was fine, the Managing Director thought ten a month was required. From looking at the data it was clear that about seven a month would bring in the growth the company was looking for (based on past results) and so they were finally able to agree on a number that looked good.

I'm not suggesting that you use this approach to beat up your staff (should that thought be going through your head). I am suggesting that you use it to help clarify and define areas of an individual's work that aren't up to scratch. Clarification of expectations can often be enough to see an upturn in an individual's performance.

Choice

The way that you apply your operational visions is, of course, up to you. A combination of all three levels (business, departmental and individual) serves most of the clients I work with and could be a good mix for you too.

A broad picture being painted for the business, with a detailed vision for the individual areas that are under-performing and supportive explanations of what good looks like for members of your teams that are struggling with their current roles is a powerful combination.

I'm sure that you'll intuitively know what would work for your organisation, so I'll leave that decision making up to you.

Recap

- You can apply the question 'what does good look like' to different levels in your business.
- Business level - high level view of what performance should look like.
- Departmental level - how the functions should work properly, and with each other.
- Individual level - what a good day looks like and what standards need to be achieved for a specific team member.

- Decide on what combinations of visioning approach and levels you need to focus on right now.

Part 2

Putting these ideas into action and designing a business that constantly moves toward its vision

The Now

This part of the book is focused on helping you to get from where you are now, to where you want to be. The ideas in this section of the book can be used independently of the ideas I shared with you in part one, should you need to do so.

To summarise what I am going to take you through during this part of the book, I will:

- Ensure that you know where you are right now.
- Help you create a plan to get you from A (where you are now) to B (where you want to be).
- Share with you some ideas to help you make the journey a shorter one.
- Explain to you how you can help coax / enforce the right kinds of behaviours to move you along your path.

Let's get started with defining your current reality, so that you have a good starting point for your journey.

Getting a grip of now

Where are you right now?

Is your business in a good place?

Are you wanting to make some minor changes, or are you

looking for a complete overhaul?

Do you have target areas to address quickly?

Do you have longer term objectives that need some focus and attention to move them along, right now?

If you have used any of methods detailed in part one of this book you may well have a list of things that don't work or just aren't present in your business. Just as you articulated a future for your business to head to, you have the opportunity to describe where you are today. I'm not suggesting that you create a 'problem statement' for your business, more a narrative of where you are today. A few bullet points highlighting the good and bad points of your business can do wonders to get conversations started on this topic.

Defining a datum

Knowing where you are right now is essential so that your plan to reach your vision is effective. For example, the direction you take to drive from your home to the next city will be different than for someone else that lives in a different part of the country. Your plan to get from A to B will likewise be different based on where you are starting from. The business with great stock control systems will have a different journey from one that doesn't have this present within their business, should they have inventory issues ham-stringing their performance.

The other main reason that I want you to be clear about where you are right now is so that you can reflect on the journey that you have travelled. This is especially useful when the going gets tough and motivation wanes. Just the other week a new director slated one of my client's managers for a low level of performance in their production facility. When the full picture of where they had been and where they had gotten to was described, a different conversation ensued. This is not to suggest that we need to let people off the hook with poor performance, but it does help to keep the bigger picture in mind during the journey itself.

Describing where you are and defining a start point helps with planning and reflection, but what about other facts and figures?

Describing now

Are there any anecdotes that you have about your current level of performance? Are there any stories that summarise the way things are today? A little story that reflects on where the business is can be a lot more powerful than pages and page of descriptive text. What stories do you have in your business? These stories can become your 'monuments of change' later on, once you have permanently remedied these situations. Let me give you an example.

A business that I used to work at as an engineer had a high level of machine breakdowns and no instances of planned maintenance. I was reliably informed that we were unable to plan downtime for our machines as our production schedule was so pressured that it just wasn't possible. Long story short, I managed to convince my manager that having some agreed downtime that was expected was better than having unexpected downtime that was actually longer than the planned alternative (I had facts and figures to back up my views). This is a perfect example of defining what good looks like and it helped our business to become more productive and more effective. Whenever a subsequent issue arose in the business where someone said that the solution wasn't possible we were able to refer back to how we overcame the planned maintenance issue and this allowed the new conversation to move from being stuck to moving once more.

What stories and anecdotes do you have in your business that could become a monument of change later on?

Highlight the quick win areas

Amongst your current issues and concerns will be a number of 'quick win' areas, identify these and demarcate them within your overall action plan that you will produce shortly.

Quick wins have a number of benefits, apart from the results that they are meant to produce. So, apart from improving, or fixing, an element of your business what else can quick wins do for your business?

- Improve the visibility of change being a good thing for your business.
- Develop momentum and confidence within your team.
- Pave the way for future improvements.
- Start to normalise change in your business (ultimately affecting the culture).
- Achieve some immediate results that promotes and reinforces your wider plan.

Quick wins are often thought about only at the start of a project, but the act of stopping and thinking about what quick wins are available in the business at this moment in time can usually produce a list of wins there and then. Plans change as new insights and facts arise; there will always be some quick wins available to you – if you decide to look for them.

If you need to reinvigorate your improvement activities at any point in time, look for the quick wins. It is a simple strategy, but because of the benefits I have just listed they can really help a team to progress. I want you to use quick wins to get a boost to your activities and develop enough momentum that you will be able to see all of your changes through.

In the next chapter I will take you through a planning sequence to help you move from where you are today, to where you want to be (a place that good looks like!).

Recap

- Identify target areas in your business if you need to focus your efforts on some short-term changes.
- Be realistic about where you are starting from and make a record for future reference (so you can see how far you have come).
- Define the quick wins that will give your team the motivation to press on and generate some results now.

The Future

The title of this section might be a little misleading… after all you know where you are going to – you have a vision!

This chapter covers a number of planning considerations that I would like you to reflect on. My intention is that you put your vision into context for where your business is and how quickly it needs to get to where you want it to be. The next chapter will look at some very practical action planning activities, but for now let us look at these considerations.

Milestones

Unless your vision is only a minor shift from where you are today it is unlikely that you will reach your destination in one small leap. Considering the milestones that your journey will pass during your journey can make it easier to plan for the ascent.

Using milestones is a great communication tool with your colleagues, your team and your superiors too. I feel confident that you will have used milestones in your working life before you picked up this book, but still I would like you to think about them in terms of your vision.

Do you need to break up your journey into a series of milestone markers that you will be able to experience on your way?

Milestones aren't essential to your plan but can really help to clarify your thoughts on how you want to scale the vision 'mountain' that you have created.

Stages and phases

A different take on milestones is that of stages and phases.

With milestones it often conjures images of passing the scenery once. But, what if the journey is more of a cyclical nature and you need to revisit an area, or topic, a number of times?

Let me give you a quick example. The owner of a small business was struggling with their product development activities. Their day-to-day work was in chaos and this was impeding the creation of the new products and services (which were vital to the future of the business). We split up their improvement approach into a number of phases, each one building on the previous one (but visiting the same ground each time). As a summary these phases covered:

- Tiny steps of progress with their service creation

activities and mopping up the current mess.

- Small steps of progress with their service creation work and also implementing effective administrative systems.
- Full blown service creation workshops with their team, running of effective business systems and sales development activities.
- Service creation streamlining, leveraging distribution channels and improving the efficiency of the business systems.

Many could argue that this is a semantic debate (milestones could be just another way of stating phases), but the thinking can be different. Thinking of your change programme as both a one trip linear plan and also a virtuous circle can provide different ways of thinking about your plans and give you a different outcome than just thinking in one way alone.

Try both on for size and see what you think about your approach to achieve your vision.

Deliverables for your stakeholders

Who is sitting behind your change programme? Are there superiors in your organisation that you need to consider? What are their needs and wants that need to be satisfied by the changes that you need to make?

Considering who is surrounding your project and what they might need to see / feel / experience as a result of your activities can change the way that you approach your project. If you need ongoing support to your project, and potentially need additional resources longer term, then giving your stakeholders what they need early on (or at least a little bit of it) can help earn goodwill for later on.

I recall a project where over thirty stakeholders were identified. Some were direct management staff to the team in question, some were several layers removed. It was an interesting exercise, but the primary stakeholder was the person directly evaluated for the performance and output of this team. This dose of reality allowed the team to narrow their focus to make sure this one person got what they needed first along with an ongoing drip feed of personal-to-them results for the duration of the project.

There's no rocket science with this example, but a good example of the 80/20 rule in practice for this consideration. A few people will need most of the results that you generate, so make sure that you keep them happy.

Know who needs what from your change project and factor this in to your plans.

Really – what does good look like?

Now that you have had some time to reflect on your operational vision, does it still look good?

Before you leap into your planning stage, let me ask you to have another look at your vision and check that it still looks good. In fact, better than good. Does it look amazing?

If it doesn't, what would the next step up from good look like? Can you articulate this and embellish what you have already defined?

Answer this question and when you are happy with your answer let me ask you to take one more consideration.

Practical future

The last consideration I would like you to undertake is about where your business is right now.

Have you tried a business wide change in the past?

What happened? Did it work out OK, or did it flop?

I don't want to temper your operational vision, but I do want you to be realistic about how the people in your business will react to the change. I have a number of strategies to help you put the changes into effect, but how much hard work will it be to help your team through the process?

This consideration really puts the other considerations into context. With this in mind, do you need different milestones or phases to help with your implementation?

As I said just a moment ago, I have some approaches in two chapters time to help you with the implementation. For now, just keep this in mind and let us move on to the planning stage.

Recap

- Determine what milestones would be useful for your change project and make a note of them for your project planning activities.

- Consider breaking your project down in phases, or stages, to make the management of the project more tangible.

- Figure out what deliverables your stakeholder(s) would want to experience and build them into your plan.

- Reflect on past improvement projects and temper your plan based on how good you currently are at making change happen (a good plan and some results is better than an overly ambitious plan and no results).

The Change

Now we're getting to point where I want you to plan the change for your business. It is well known that the majority of change programmes fall over. This chapter of the book is designed to help you plan your change, the next chapter will share with you some ideas to help you evolve the way that your business operates by helping to shape the habits that are held within it. For now, let us look at some of the key ingredients of making the change you want to stick become a reality.

Getting a team together

Are you going to deliver this change on your own?

I hope not. I hope that you have some people around you, to complement your skills, that can help you with your journey.

Do you know who these people are, the ones that can help you?

As I write these words I am thinking of the people I partnered up with in the past to make change happen; some partnerships worked really well, and some didn't.

I have tried to make change happen on my own too. Sometimes

this has been the right thing to do and sometimes it hasn't. Learning is key to making change happen more effectively over the longer term (I'll come back to this point in a later chapter) and thankfully, I'd like to think, I have learned from my mistakes. You probably already have your views on this topic; please bring your experiences to the table when you are implementing change!

Having a team is really helpful when you get stuck, overwhelmed, confused, sidetracked, seconded, lost or anything else that stops you from travelling in a straight line to the goal you have chosen. It is natural to experience all of these feelings and with a colleague or two accompanying you it becomes easier to get out of your 'funk' when it happens.

Choosing who you team up with is vitally important. Do you know what skills are required (that perhaps you do not have)? Can you find people that have the right skills for the task in hand? Can you work well with these people? Don't just choose friends, include friendly co-workers that can help you execute your plan.

There might also need to be other people that need to join your team, in different roles to help the project along. You might want a mentor to help you reflect and navigate a route when the going gets tough. You might want a sponsor for when the project gets tricky and you need some obstacles taken out of your way. What about suppliers? You might need someone that can deliver something for your team to join the party?

When choosing your team, you may also want to consider how you will communicate. If this is a new group of people working together you might need a formal system of communication agreed in advance. If you are used to working together then you may not need something so sophisticated, perhaps just a good action plan will be enough in this situation.

There are entire books written on team dynamics and choosing project teams, unfortunately this is out of the scope of this book. I hope that the above pointers will give you some food for thought as you think through who you will work with in order to deliver your changes (and if you personally get on well with your team mates, all the better!).

Creating an action plan

Your action plan is your next item to consider; what are your team going to be working on?

There are lots of recommendations on how to create a good action plan, and even though this is largely outside of the scope of this book, let me give you a few pointers.

B to A

If you are fortunate enough to know what needs to go into your action plan, please move on to the next sub-section. If, however, you are not entirely sure how you will get from where you are to where you want to be the 'B to A' method could help.

Most people plan out their action steps by thinking what they need to do next, and then the step after that etc... In my experience of working with people that get stuck with their action plans they seem to have a fairly good grip of what their immediate tasks are, but no idea of how to close the gap of the actions to get them to the end of the project... it just dissolves into a cloud with a question mark on it.

An alternative way to plan is to start at the end (with the objective having been achieved) and imagine your way back to your present situation. The linking question is 'because I'd...' and you use this to link your objective back to its penultimate action and then keep repeating until you end up at today.

For example:

I have reached my objective of implementing an effective business planning cycle, because I'd...

Validated that the method work, because I'd...

Operated the cycle for three months, because I'd...

Trained my staff in how the use the cycle, because I'd...

Documented how the cycle works, because I'd...

Agreed with my team what the cycle was, because I'd...

Mapped out what needed to go into the cycle, because I'd...

Agreed the specification of the cycle, because I'd...

Spoken to the stakeholders of the process, because I'd...

Aligned the cycle with other business processes, because I'd...

Been clear about what the cycle had to achieve, because I'd...

Had a kick off meeting with the business' CEO.

It might take a few goes to get the hang of the method, but it can be a great tool to generate a path. Reversing it, juggling the steps and adding in any other items that spring to mind can then transform your 'B to A' plan into a really comprehensive 'A to B' plan that will achieve the results you want. This method is also really good if you are new to an area / objective that requires planning. Imagination and common sense can take your planning a long way.

5W1H

Can you recall the 5W1H method I shared with you earlier in this book? This is the prompt for "What, When, Where, Who, Why and How". If you take the majority of these you have the elements required to capture your action plan. A simple spreadsheet using these as prompts for headings can take you a long way.

Let me run through the headings that I would normally include for an action plan:

- Action reference (serial number 01, 02, 03 etc…).
- **What** the action is.
- **Who** is responsible for completing the action (not necessarily carrying out the action).
- **When** the task is due.
- **How** the action is to be closed out (the deliverable), if required for the task.
- The status of the task (live, complete, on hold etc…).
- Any notes about the task that will help with its completion.

Using a spreadsheet to record the tasks is an effective way to capture and filter the actions by their due date and status as you progress through the changes. Of course, with the surge in online task management tools there are plenty of options to consider. Finding an approach that you are comfortable using is vital as regular updates and monitoring will make all of the difference to your change project.

Kaizen

Hopefully you will recognise the reference 'Kaizen', often described as a Japanese word for continuous improvement. Kaizen is a great technique to help beat procrastination on change projects through the utilisation of small steps. Small steps help to avoid us triggering our own 'fight or flight' response, which in the context of change projects leads to change not happening at all.

From a planning point of view we can use the Kaizen principle to help us ensure that our plans are going to be 'comfortable' for our team members as we ease them gently into this period of change. You will most likely have experienced this before; you want to make a change in the business, you are happy with what needs to happen (you have been planning it for weeks or months) and when you share it with your team they freak out.

Progress is minimal, and results are negligible. Kaizen can help to remedy this situation.

I recall a Team Leader working on a project in their factory who was getting no buy-in from his team. He knew what we wanted and how he wanted it done. The problem in this situation was that his team hadn't slowly immersed themselves in this challenge for the last few weeks, this was new to them. Whereas the Team Leader had been able to slowly bathe himself in the early days of the project this was a sharp shock to the team themselves. We used the Kaizen principle to break down the first few elements of the project so that they weren't so onerous. Once the team realised that all the Team Leader was asking them to do was a handful of small tasks they started to get on with the project actions.

This is how it often happens. A project that has stalled has its first few actions broken down into microscopic 'tid bits' (and, if in doubt – go smaller!) and action re-starts. Confidence grows and momentum builds. The later actions get eaten up whole and the project cruises through to completion. Kaizen is brilliant for helping your team to become more confident with handling change and shouldn't be overlooked.

In the context of this book I want to make sure that you are aware of the Kaizen principle (small steps helping to build confidence and momentum) and that you consider breaking up the first few steps of your action plan to help take advantage of this approach.

PDCA

Like Kaizen, it is highly likely that you either use, or have come across PDCA. Just to make sure, PDCA is an acronym for Plan, Do, Check and Act. It is also known as the continuous improvement cycle and for many businesses its power is underutilised. The last two points in this chapter have been directed at the Plan stage, obviously you and your team will need to Do some work in order to execute the Plan, but what then?

Most businesses will move on quickly from task to task, ticking off items from their action plan without mulling over the consequences of the actions. The Check segment allows you to reflect on the effectiveness of the action and the Act segment is an opportunity for you to determine how you want to change your approach (if required). It isn't passive, it is an active way to manage your actions and I want you to consider it in light of your improvement action plan.

Whether you want to build this in to your action plan format I will leave up to you. Depending on how my clients at the time are faring I may well introduce these elements into the action plan template by adding in the following items to the list I mentioned under the 5W1H sub-section of this chapter:

- Outcome (Check).
- Change in approach? (Act).

Having these two additional columns can make a big difference to the way your team approach the challenge of the plan. As I said just a moment ago, this is about moving people away from mechanically closing off tasks and into thinking about what they are doing. There is little point in just ticking off the tasks if you have realised that the task is ineffective and you should have done something else, or need to complete a related task.

Proper sign offs

When is a project, or task, 'done' in your eyes?

This is a question that you should ask yourself as you plan out either the main change project, or the sub-projects that make up the overall programme. I have seen many projects that just about make it, only to have a wobble at the very end and nearly not make it because of this issue (they do make it because I, or a member of my client's staff have intervened, of course!).

So, how do you currently close off the actions and projects you run in your business? I want you to have a think about this and come up with an answer before you start planning your project. The simplest approach is to gain agreement with a key stakeholder of your project before you start as to what they want to see at the end of the project. Without a formal signoff you run the risk of not completing your project, but just stopping without any benefit.

The 'what does good look like?' question is perfect for this element. What does your key stakeholder want to experience at the successful completion of the project? Ask them, record it and then agree to meet their expectations. Generically speaking the end of the project, their sign off point, is likely to be a couple of steps after where you may have thought the project will have finished. This is one of the benefits of agreeing a proper sign off for the project; you all end up in the right place at the right time.

If you want to do some thinking, before you ask a stakeholder for their sign off requirements, imagine the future and let your mind flow over the business after you walk away from the project and ask yourself these questions:

- Will there any unfinished business?
- Will the gains be sustained after my involvement has ceased?
- Are there any training, or maintenance, tasks that I have left out of this project?
- Will all documentation have been completed by the end of the project?
- What is the risk of a 'relapse' after the project has concluded?

Think this through and ensure that your project has a robust close out activity before you get started.

Visibility

Where will you keep your action plan once it has been created?

Will you be making it visible and easy to review when progress is to be discussed, or will it be tucked away on the hard drive of your computer?

Making a project plan visible can make a big difference to the progress made on it. If it is in your face then there is a good chance that you will look at it. If you look at it then there is a good chance that you will take action. If you look at it then there is a chance that others will look at it too.

This may be one of the simplest strategies that you can employ to help ensure that a project makes progress, but it is also one of the best returns on effort that you can undertake when it comes to making change happen.

Can you find a wall space that you can dedicate to displaying your action plan? Can you agree on a visual method for identifying the status of tasks? Can you link your regular team meetings to the plan and ensure that your plan becomes part of those meetings?

Hiding your plans away is a risky strategy for most of us and doesn't naturally lead to progress when the busy-ness of the working day takes over.

Consider how you will constantly (or as constantly as practical) keep your project in the minds of your team and think of other ways that you can make your projects (and their immediate actions to complete) visible in your business.

Timings, resources and sequences

When you look at your plan, does it look right?

I am not going to get into critical path analysis with this comment, more that I want you to think through the steps in your action plan and feel comfortable that the flow of the actions look and feel right.

From a timings perspective; do the deadlines look appropriate to the needs of the business, the workloads of the people working on the activities and the overall success of the project?

From a resources perspective; do you have the right tasks on the right people at the right time, or is it overloaded in some areas?

From a sequence perspective; are the activities linked in a logical manner that allows for the most effective and efficient route to the finish line?

These might seem to be basic considerations, but a quick glance over your project action plan (before commencing) with these three considerations can often yield observations that can be built into the programme and improve the final result. Think of this as a pause before you attempt lift off, similar to the approach space agencies take at mission control just before they ignite the engines.

Support and sponsorship

We've talked about the team that you are going to be involved with, to complete the tasks that are on your action plan, but do you need some additional support? I am talking about mentors, sponsors and advisors that could help you to kick down obstacles when you need help and to keep you accountable during the life of the project.

Many projects fade away for both of these reasons. If the going gets too tough, on top of your normal job responsibilities, the improvement plan could end up on the scrap heap. If you aren't held accountable for the delivery of this particular project then the next 'shiny' project that comes along could vie for your attention and has a chance to win.

Throughout my career, both as an employee and as a

consultant, I have found having both of these facets covered to be invaluable. I don't know everything and I don't always have access to knowledge and resources that other people do; being able to tap into them during an improvement project can make all the difference between being covered in glory and… well, you get the picture.

Is there someone in your organisation that would be willing to help you with both of these items (to help you and keep you accountable) and is in a position to be able to do something, should the going get tough? If you know of someone (or, it could be a few people that all have complementary skills), it is worth having a conversation to see if you can line them up for the start of your change project.

What does good look like for your project?

I have just about finished my additional thoughts on delivering a programme of change for your organisation, but there is one final question I would like to ask you:

What does good look like for the project you are about to undertake?

If you reflect on your past projects, good and bad, you will most likely have some preferences for how you want this next project to fare.

What would you like to avoid and what would you like to have more of?

What would you like to experience with your change projects that you haven't in the past?

From the way that your team integrate with each other and embrace the ideas you are implementing, you get to have a say in how the project unfolds. From defining how you want your team meetings to be run, who updates the project plan, how formal / informal various features of the project are, you can make a mark on how the project itself is delivered.

Do you want short team huddles to kick out the obstacles from the project, where the participants stand up next to a whiteboard with the project tasks on it?

Do you want a sit-down meeting, once a month, to discuss the plans?

Do you want your stakeholders and sponsors to attend the occasional team meeting, or something more formal?

Would you like a weekly catch up with your mentor to review progress and to ask for advice (with the option to cancel if you feel OK with where you are)?

"What does good look like?" can be applied to a wide range of topics and defining the standards for your improvement project is no different. Let me move on to the next chapter and I'll share with you some ideas on how to improve the habits your business needs to live and breathe in order to fulfil your operational vision.

Recap

- Assemble your team.
- When developing your plan consider the B to A approach, 5W1H, Kaizen, PDCA, including proper sign offs and keeping your plans visible.
- Review your plan to make sure it looks right - timings, resources and the overall sequence of tasks.
- Consider getting some support and sponsorship for your project, for when things get tough and to avoid

progress slowing.

The New Habits

Now we get to a fascinating phenomenon – habits.

We all know that good habits are essential to making change happen; there are countless books written about habits and how to acquire them. How is this working out for your business so far?

I am going to offer you a slightly different way to develop habits in your business, through design rather than self-control. This section of the book looks at three distinct areas; Killer Questions, Metrics and Review Horizons.

It is my intention that once you have read this section you can build in some of these ideas into your improvement plan.

Killer Questions

The term 'killer questions' came from one of my clients. I had drawn out a list of questions that were to be either answered 'yes' or 'no'. No narrative, no stories, no supporting information. The questions were focused on key parts of their business process and were used to great effect to focus people on the right activities (which of course means that the questions need to be balanced out for the operations of your business).

The process of creating killer questions is relatively straightforward:

- Review your key business process* and identify critical points in the process.
- For each critical point create a question that proper execution yields a 'yes' answer.
- Look at your regular meetings and attach the questions to the appropriate meetings.
- Assign the questions to those responsible and tell them what additional work you want them to do if the answer is 'no'. This additional information tells the person running the meeting how your process step will get back on track and what effect the 'no' has on the business.
- Hold the meetings, as per your normal business routine, and act on the information as appropriate.

* And don't forget that you can use your operational vision to help establish what should be happening and the questions that you should be asking!

To get you started I have an example list of questions to help you form your own questions. These questions are linked to the utopia statements we saw earlier in this book.

Goods Inward

- Have all of the expected deliveries arrived?
- Have all of the deliveries been booked in and located?
- Is the QC inspection queue cleared?

Stores

- Are the PI counts 100% accurate?
- Do all pallets have batch labels?

Picking

- Have all of the due picks been delivered to Production?
- Have all stock discrepancies been dealt with?

Sales Orders

- Have all new sales orders been loaded?
- Have all sales invoice issues been resolved?
- Are there any outstanding customer queries / complaints?
- Is the sales order book aligned with our agreed delivery dates?

- Are the forecasts up to date?

Works Orders / Planning

- Have all of the works order MRP suggestions been actioned?
- Is the works order book in line with our sales orders?
- Have all works order been launched on time?
- Is the capacity plan accurate?
- Are there any capacity 'blips' that need to be addressed?
- Have all works orders started on time?
- Have ECN works order / purchase order deletions (and re-creation) happened?

Purchase Orders

- Have all of the purchasing MRP suggestions been actioned?
- Are our replenishment setting appropriate for our current supply chains / production volumes?

Shop Floor Data Collection

- Are all trained operators booking operations correctly?
- Is the work to list's sequence being followed?

Engineering

- Have all agreed structure (BoM and route) changes been made?
- Are our BoMs accurate?

General

- Have the agreed housekeeping routines been executed?

Killer questions are a great way to convert the design of your new process activities into day to day action. You might experience a lot of 'no's the first few days of trying this out, but with the right support and the right engagement with your team this can soon become primarily 'yes' answers and your business performance will soar.

Metrics

How you measure your business' operations makes a big difference to the activities that are undertaken and the results you achieve. If you are wanting to help shape how your team behave and operate then having the right types, distribution and ownership of measures is seriously worth spending some time considering.

This section of the book will rapidly run through this area and intends to give you some ideas on what you can do in your own business to help get the effect you want. The right measures can direct your team into living and breathing the new vision as part of their normal working day.

Process Metrics

There are many ways to measure your business activities and process driven measures make a lot of sense, especially if you have been re-designing how you want your business processes to operate. Considering your metrics as input, process and output metrics can help you to get the right measures for the right people at the right time.

Many businesses will only consider 'ouput' metrics, telling you a story of what happened in the process. These are useful and can help you to reflect and develop your business, but in some cases limit the ability for a business to perform to its full potential. 'Input' metrics can be really useful to help you gauge what is happening with the start of the process, and whether it is being triggered correctly. Like the output metrics you can use this information to help you decide on how you want to improve next time around. However, unlike output metrics, you can also change tack there and then and use the information to influence a different outcome. For most of us, wanting to exert change into our businesses, measuring and acting upon this type of information is one of the quickest ways to make some quick gains. By identifying input metrics, making them part of the daily work discussion, linking responsibility to individuals and acting upon the information, you can dramatically improve your results.

The other type of metric, process, is similar to the input metrics with one small difference. Depending on where you are in the process itself will determine how much control you have over the outcome of your process. Input metrics may well involve a supplier (internal or external to your business), whereas the process metrics will reflect directly on what you and your team are doing at this moment in time. Process metrics are the closest thing you will have to the dashboard of your car. Want to go faster? Press the accelerator pedal. Want to go slower? Press the brake pedal. I'm sure that you get the idea.

When you get a better mix of metrics you can start to use them to empower the people around you. They can begin to measure and manage what they are doing and to exert influence on the outcome. Business results doesn't have to be a fait accompli!

Temporary and permanent

To get a change in your team you may need to consider having a balance of temporary and permanent measures in place. There will be some fundamental measures that you will want to always have in place (e.g. safety, profit, on time delivery, quality, costs etc...), but there will also be some temporary measures that you would like to have in place.

Temporary measures are exactly that, something that you need to focus on until the actions that produce the result become a habit. Once the habit has started, you can consider dropping the measure and only reinstate it when the performance in that area requires additional support (but hopefully it will not, of course). Temporary measures are useful when there are new starters joining a team and measuring something relevant helps them to identify if they are doing the job right.

Some temporary measures will last over time and find a place in the overall collection of KPIs, but don't feel that you have to keep a measure going if the results are constantly good and the performance measure wraps up into a higher-level measure (I'll come back to this in a moment). Measures are a means to an end; if you don't like what they are telling you, change what you are doing.

To put temporary measures into action, simply list out the issues you are facing (that prevent you from reaching your vision), determine an appropriate way to state the results of that issue and measure and report on them as you change the activity that is taking place until you get the results. When you hit an agreed level of performance for a period of time you can then retire the measure.

For staff members that are a little reluctant with change, agreeing on when a measure can be stopped (if you do this, we can stop measuring that) can be a motivator to start doing the right things. By the time that the performance levels have been reached it is highly likely that benefits have been realised and the individual(s) in question will have at least seen that your proposed change was a good idea. As with all people related issues around change – some will get onboard and some won't. This strategy can help to get people on board.

Digital and Analogue

Metrics don't have to come in percentage form all of the time. When you are trying to form new habits it might be that you need to simply get a feel for how often a task has been completed in line with your vision. To keep this demarcation clear I refer to analogue metrics being things that can be measured on a scale (such as supplier on time delivery) and digital metrics refer to activities that are either present or not (such as holding a meeting, or not).

Some metrics will be easy to measure in a (more traditional) analogue way. Data will be available for you to crunch and produce some useful numbers; percentages, ratios and absolute values being the most common. The speedometer on the dashboard of your car is a great example. The number will mean something and it is highly likely that you have specified what good looks like for these numbers (aka your targets). As I write this I have a client that is measuring the lead time through one of their processes and they have established that five days would be a good target to hit, so we are measuring the lead time in days whilst keeping an eye on the target.

Other metrics will make more sense if they are simply 'yes / no' measures. Discrete activities will take place and you will be able to capture them as to whether they took place, or whether they produced a result. Going back to the car dashboard analogy, it is similar to the oil light. When you have a problem the light comes on; it is either on or off. A current client of mine is trying to establish a daily team meeting for one of their logistics functions. At the end of the week the Team Leader reports back to the manager on a number of items and one of them is how many times the meeting ran that week. The other elements of the reporting can help to tell if the meeting was effective or not, but this number (of times the meeting has been executed) tells the manager if the team are making the effort to get together and review their standard agenda. Over time, and compounded by good results, this meeting will become a habit and the metric will most likely become redundant.

Have a look at the metrics you currently have and see if you have an effective balance between analogue and digital measures.

Cascaded and relevant

The final point I will make about metrics is that many organisations develop them in a very one-dimensional way, one suite of measures that the top management use. This is a good place to start but having different measures at different levels in the business can help your teams to behave and operate in the way that your vision requires. Metrics must be relevant to the people involved with them.

For example, one of my clients has a bagging operation. The management team talk about profit margins, quality and delivery performance. It was only after we shared with the bagging plant operatives their 'bags per hour' score that they could find meaning in the other numbers. The other three scores were a step away from where they were and consequently meaningless. Their bagging rates were largely in their control and therefore they were able to influence the outcome.

A related point here is the setting of targets, or what I often refer to as 'reasonable expectations'. There is no issue with using the word target with your team, for many it will work well. The reason I like the term reasonable expectations is that it instantly gives the feeling that it has been thought through and isn't some ridiculous figure plucked out of thin air (unlike when a Finance Director once asked for raw material stock targets to be less than minimum working capital…). Reasonable expectations are something that you can talk about, work towards and exceed, as part of your ongoing conversations about realising the vision that has been established.

Metrics are a great way to help drive the right behaviours and develop the right kinds of habits. From this section I hope that you can take away a few points that can help bolster your approach to making your vision a sustainable reality.

Reporting lines

Another consideration to undertake as you reflect on your action plan is what reporting lines you currently have in your business. Some businesses have already embraced a healthy mix of informal and formal reporting lines throughout the structure of their organisation.

When I talk to my clients about formal reporting, it is often met with a groan. Well, initially at least. Once the discussion of just how light it can be and in what format formal reporting can take place, my clients usually move from groaning to interest. The realisation that for a small investment in time you can garner excellent business information to make informed decisions is welcomed. When they actually put this into practice and start getting positive results their interest now moves to advocacy – why wouldn't they want to carry on with this?

Formal reporting can take the format of regular written reports, presentations at agreed intervals, weekly email updates, one to one meetings (with a fixed agenda), agenda items at routine management meetings, visual management systems and more. If you don't use some of these vehicles then it might be worth re-looking at the behaviours and habits that you want to demonstrate in your business and then consider linking them to your formal reporting.

How far down the line should you go with formal reporting? I believe that every layer of the organisation has at least some element of formal reporting lines present. If you want to cascade the 'what good looks like' standards through your business then you need some kind of mechanism to communicate this in both directions. The standards need to flow down the organisation and formal reporting back up, in a closed loop performance cycle arrangement.

Informal reporting usually takes care of itself, hence the name. My only comment on this is that if you, as a leader in your organisation, are not being adequately kept abreast of what is going on and are not witnessing habits being reinforced, slowly move your informal reporting over to formal. Remember, there needs to be a payoff between the two; the formal reporting has got to yield a greater return than the effort / time it takes to produce and review the reporting.

If there are members of your business who do not have a formal reporting line, to report how they are doing in relation to the standards (or, reasonable expectations) they are being measured against, please consider helping them by putting something in place. Organising this can be as simple as deciding what you want to know (to help you fulfil your vision), when you want it, from whom and in what format.

What does good look like for your formal reporting?

Routines

The word routines is often taken as another word for habits. In business this is especially true; formally setting out and agreeing your routines can help set the tempo for the team and reinforce what needs to happen in order to achieve the end result.

Routines can help translate parts of your vision into day to day activity, bridging the gap of how you get from A to B. Cause and effect thinking can be a useful approach to take when thinking about making a shift in your performance; routines are great when they are focused on activities that generate specific outcomes (in this case, your vision).

It is highly likely that you will already have some routines (informal, or formal) and that you can build upon them. This might be regular team meetings, reporting cycles, end of month accounts, external auditing activities and so on. What I am suggesting here is that you consider your operational vision, look at the new activities that you will need to engage with consistently and then drawing out a routine for your business.

I am not suggesting that you translate your routines into a minute-by-minute breakdown of the working day, more a list of what actions need to be completed on which days. If you want to develop the idea further you can add in who has ownership of which task too. The important thing about the routine is that you capture all of the tasks that your business needs to perform and draw them out. Some quick action points here include:

- List out all of the tasks that you need to routinely perform in order to live your new vision (these will likely be linked to your business process and probably not your action plan).
- Decide on the frequency of each task; daily, weekly, monthly, quarterly etc...
- Assign ownership to each task (this is the person responsible for making sure the routine task is executed and works, not necessarily the person who will do the

task).

- Draw out your routines so that everyone can see what needs to be done when.
- Trial the routine, iron out any bugs and then keep going!

Tying the routine into your normal daily / weekly management meetings (or, team huddles) can help you to see what is and isn't being completed in a timely fashion. Knowing this helps you to understand if you are on track or whether your team need support (in terms of either education or physical resource to help deal with workloads).

A good routine can make all of the difference when it comes to improving the performance of your team. The idea of formalising a routine can make a lot of managers feel uneasy due to the connotations of dictating what needs to be done when. There are two ways of looking at this:

1. This is part of the job of management.
2. You can involve your team in developing the routine, so that it is less painful for them (and hopefully, actually embraced).

Either way, a good routine is certainly worth considering when looking for options to embed your new operational vision.

Formal Reviews

The final option I would like to discuss in this chapter wraps up the previous items. Holding formal reviews can help bring together the items:

- Killer questions
- Metrics
- Routines
- Reporting Lines

Having a time out from the day-to-day busyness to look at all of these (or whatever combination you opted for) can really help you to spot opportunities for improvement.

A regular time slot with a standard agenda is the key to making this approach work. The meetings don't have to be long, just long enough to ensure that you cover the main points, review any actions from previous meetings and capture any new actions that you need to see happen.

If you are sitting there thinking 'great, another task to add to my busy to-do list!', here's an option for you. If this book is about moving to a vision of performance, how would you like this event to happen? What would good look like in this situation?

Typically, the manager would write down the actions and make the notes, leading the session. What if your team were responsible for preparing the notes, organising the session and handling the subsequent actions? It is only a minor shift in approach, but one that should help you to handle the staff you have in your team. You would need to agree some rules to this, to ensure that you are happy with the outcome (such as signing off the list of actions after the meeting and being able to comment on any things that aren't going as expected), but it is a possibility. This way round it means that everyone takes part, sharing the kinds of habits that you would want in your business, and you don't become burdened by yet another management task.

Regular reviews are an essential element to keeping your business activities on track and to the standard that is required. You can develop the agenda to ensure that all of the standards you want to see in your business are present, that the routines are being executed to the agreed timescales, that the metrics are showing the results that you want to witness and that the reporting is appropriate. If the situation isn't as you would have hoped for then you have the opportunity to speak up and re-direct.

At first these meetings could take some time, I don't want to paint you a rosy picture unnecessarily. If you are trying to shift your business' culture by a number of degrees it is likely that you will have a range of loose ends that need to be corrected, which will extend across the first couple of meetings until there is a resolution to the issues. Once you have gotten on top of matters then you can look to streamline the meetings, possibly dropping some of the agenda items and only re-introducing them if there is a relapse in performance.

Another consideration is the frequency of these meetings. It might be that once you are up and running that having these meetings at three or six monthly intervals would be appropriate. But, depending on where you are starting from, you may choose to have the first few on a weekly basis to make sure that you have enough momentum to get through the list of corrections you want to make in the business. You will have a feel for this but, if in doubt, do more early on!

Pick your options

The intention of this section of the book was to share with you some options that could augment your plan and improve the way that habits form in your business. Forming habits is one of the trickier parts of moving from where you are today to where you want to be. Repetition has a strong place in forming new habits and hopefully the approaches that I shared with you in the past few pages will be ones that you will be able to adopt and integrate with your action plan.

I recommend that you take another look at your action plan and consider building in the approaches from this chapter that resonate with you. Remember, the plan doesn't finish when you complete the tasks. The plan finishes when you have an embedded series of habits that deliver the results you want and operates in a way that aligns with your vision!

Recap

- Review your business processes and develop some yes / no 'killer questions', to help ensure your team know what needs to happen every day and week. Add the questions to your regular team meetings.
- Develop a handful of metrics that allow you to measure and adjust your main business processes.
- Share the metrics with your team and let them develop variants that are more meaningful to them, if appropriate.

- Review the organisational structure of your business and reflect on the formal reporting activities that are in place; augment / amend as you see fit.
- Formalise a 'loose' routine for your business so that everyone knows what tasks are meant to happen by when.
- Consider introducing formal reviews into your business to wrap all of the above points together.

The Implementation

At this point you should now have a highly effective plan to implement your vision and make a shift in terms of both how your business performs and feels. You can have a high level of performance that is draining, stressful and tiring but, hopefully, you have designed a future state that is productive and controlled (and generally calm).

This chapter looks at some topics that support the implementation of your plan.

Execution

Without execution nothing happens. Finding ways to make sure that your implementation activities happen is essential. Thinking your strategies through is a worthwhile exercise if you think there may be a risk of inertia.

Tiny steps can be used to great effect if the project seems too much to handle for some of your team. This approach, also known as Kaizen, is a great way to avoid the 'fight or flight' response that can take effect when the situation seems overwhelming. Nibbling away builds momentum as confidence builds. Tie this approach in with some quick wins and you have a great recipe to gain traction when you are either starting or have stalled.

Dedicated time is another strategy worth bearing in mind. It might seem hard to do, but if someone is on holiday, poorly or away on a training course your business will most likely be able to carry on (for a period of time anyway). Dedicating time to individuals, or small teams, to work on the business change activities can just be a matter of discipline and doesn't have to just come in large chunks. You can get a lot done in a short period of time if you are prepared; even ten minutes can make a difference if it is the right kind of ten minutes.

Leading on from the last point, preparation is often undervalued and underestimated in terms of how it can increase the effectiveness of delivering a change programme. Having a clear list of preparation tasks, to complement your execution tasks is another practical strategy to make sure that the gaps that appear in your diary can always be loaded with something meaningful.

Keeping the tempo of the execution is the final point I would like to raise in this section. I see many businesses that try to do too much on top of their normal obligations and, unsurprisingly, progress halts. When the strain subsides and everyone remembers what they were trying to achieve, progress starts up again, only to suffer the same misfortune once again. This pattern not only sends mixed messages through your business but is highly frustrating. It is often simpler, more effective and less stressful to plan for a small amount of regular activity to take place each week and enjoy the bonus of completing the project tasks sooner if you end up with a 'good week'.

How you choose to approach the execution of your improvement project is once again subject to the question 'what does good look like?'. I trust that you will find a good fit for your business, the people in it and the other obligations you have to manage, at the same time as you are changing how the business works.

Project reviews

As your project execution takes place I urge you to consider adding some project reviews to your schedule. To make your life easy in this regard there is only one question I want you to ponder over:

How do we get our tasks back on track?

If your tasks aren't behind schedule then ignore the question, close the meeting and get on with your day. If your tasks are slipping, however, this one question can make your life a lot easier if you repeat it often enough throughout the life of your project.

Many business managers seem to fear the idea of slippage and hope that somehow things will straighten out at the end. Pixie dust rarely works for these managers and I want to ensure that you don't get stuck down the same cul-de-sac as they do by ensuring that you hold short, effective, reviews that ensure that your change programme stays on track.

Who you want to invite to the meeting is largely a choice that is appropriate for your business. As a general rule the review meetings should be with yourself (as project lead), your key stakeholders and possibly a mentor if you have acquired one. General team reviews should be built into your project plan to ensure that your team are on track, this review is with the people that you are accountable to (assuming that you have them) to look at the bigger picture of whether the project is delivering the key benefits it was designed to achieve.

Stopping on a regular basis to take stock and to evaluate your current efforts versus results is important to make sure that you are doing the right things in order to effect the right change. As the ability to predict exactly how a project will turn out is limited for most of us this is a great opportunity to change our approach if we need to. If you subscribe to the PDCA (Plan, Do, Check and Act) model then you will recognise these review meetings as the Check and Act phases in action.

Keeping your project on track is essential to seeing it through and realising its rewards as quickly as possible. The next point is another accelerator that you can combine with this approach, but this next one is a personal approach as opposed to the group.

Learning

I touched on the PDCA model above, also known as the continuous improvement cycle. The PDCA cycle works great for improvement projects – come up with an effective Plan, Do some actions, Check your results, decide how you want to Act next (do more, do less, do something different, take a time out etc…). Alongside this is an opportunity for you to learn something about how you deliver change and how you can become more effective. Actually, this isn't just for you – it's for the whole team but let us start with you.

The model that I will share with you is a variation on the PDCA model and is called CARL, which stands for:

Challenge
Actions
Reflection
Learning

The way that you use this model is to periodically stop and consider your personal effectiveness at effecting the changes that your plan is requiring. Your project reviews should be handling the nuts and bolts of pace and progress against the tasks, but this additional review is all about how you can change your personal approach to get a better result.

Applying the model is straightforward:
- Identify an element of the project you have recently been working on (the Challenge).
- Review what Actions you undertook (and possibly which ones you didn't undertake) during this Challenge period.

- Reflect on how effective your Actions were. Did they produce the results that you wanted? What went right? What went wrong? What would you do differently? What would you avoid? What would you push for next time? Explore the results from your actions and see what observations you can make.

- The final step is to Learn from these observations. This is easier said than done (I did say straightforward and *not* easy!) and many people skirt over this the first few times they try out the approach. The Learning isn't about facts and figures it's all about how you have better understood how to navigate your situations more effectively and more efficiently in the future. If your boss doesn't like the way that you present proposals, Learn from it and change your approach. If your colleagues need to have better specifications for their tasks Learn how to write better specs. If you have seriously underestimated the time required for certain tasks and your scheduling has gone to pot, Learn from it.

The whole point of this section is to stress that you don't have to be the same person at the end of the project as you were at the start. If you don't learn something from the change project your next project will be just the same. If you don't learn from your experiences, you will find making change unpleasant and difficult and you won't want to do too much of it in the future. If you figure out what works and what doesn't, then you have the opportunity to make it bearable and perhaps even come to love the process of change and getting people onboard.

Of course, CARL doesn't just have to apply to improvement projects, so don't just use it here!

General project monitoring

In the last section I mentioned the monitoring of the general project tasks as almost a throwaway comment. I don't mean to take this lightly, but if you are reading this book there is a really good chance that you know how to manage a set of actions on a list. That said, let me share with you a few thoughts I have on the subject of the general monitoring of project tasks.

General progress should be tracked by a regular team meeting. This isn't the review meeting that I mentioned earlier in this chapter, this is the nuts and bolts review of looking at the deadlines and asking the person assigned to that task for an update on the deliverables. I will stress the need for deliverables again; being clear about what each task needs to produce will make your project much easier to manage – this is when people know what good looks like for the outcome of each of the project steps.

If there is a lack of progress, or the outcome isn't as desired, you have the opportunity to find out what support the individual requires to get them back on track. Finding out what education, resource, obstacle or skill they need help with is key here to figure out the best way to get them back on track. If there is obstinance, I will let you deal with that in your usual manner!

Setting the team up to win is really important and something that many businesses fail to do ahead of starting their projects. We have covered many of the factors for setting your team up to win in this book, but let me quickly summarise the key points to help you pull this together:

- Create a vision (of what good looks like).
- Share the vision with the team and ensure that they understand it.
- Create opportunities to keep an open conversation going about the project (such as at your project update meetings).
- Identify any obstacles that are in the way and help the team to remove them from the path.

- Have strategies in place to help your team if they get stuck (coaching, finding others with the necessary skills, resource etc…).

The only other item that I would add to this list is giving them tools and methodologies to help them become more effective and efficient at solving problems, managing their time, and escalating issues. Providing them with other practical tools that can help anyone become better at delivering their tasks are worth sharing.

The same question that I posed in the project reviews sub-section of this chapter still stands for your reviewing of project tasks – **what do you need to do to get back on track?** This question combined with everything else I have just mentioned should be able to conquer the majority of the issues you and your team will face during your implementation.

Looking for the signs

As you progress through your project you will want to keep an eye out for signs that you are moving towards your vision. Most people find that these types of projects are difficult when you consider them as a whole, but when you treat them as a series of small projects all linked together they can become more manageable.

I have mentioned quick wins a number of times in this book. Being aware of what they are in your plan and when they have been completed is a great opportunity to publicise what has been achieved and a great opportunity to let your business celebrate. Having a feeling of winning is why so many computer games are popular and we shouldn't overlook this basic reward strategy – celebrate your wins too.

The quick wins, and the feeling of winning, will help to build momentum with your changes and improve the adoption of the new habits you want to develop. Having these points of 'winning' recognised throughout your project's life will help with where you want to get to longer term and how quickly you will be able to get there.

If you aren't seeing the signs of winning, then I urge you to look at your plan again and review the sequence of steps that you have put in place to make sure that you have optimised the route that you will be taking. If the lack of progress is down to the physical activity taking place then I would ask you to look at how you are dedicating time for the work, who is being asked to do the work, the size of the work chunks and to ensure that clarity of what needs to be done when is in place. There is usually some obvious blockage in place when you look at a project like this and getting them jump started again is usually only a decision away.

Achieving and developing 'what does good look like'

At some point you will reach your vision, where what good looks like closely resembles where your business is now. Don't forget to celebrate with your team; the performance your business will now be achieving and the style in which is does it should be (considerably) different to how it was before you started.

This leads to a very logical question – what does good look like now?

Does it still look the same as when you started out on your journey, or does it look a little different now? It is highly likely that you will have learned a few things during your journey and had a few insights along the way. What you thought looked good at the start might not necessarily look as good now. You may well have had your eyes opened along the way and have now seen a better way to operate your business and team activities. This is not a problem, this is just opportunity sitting in front of you and you are now able to see this opportunity (whereas before it could have been invisible to you).

Developing what does good look like for your business is a high-level element of continuous improvement. If you were able to answer 'yes, my current situation does look good' probably means one of three things:

1. You are having a rest and need some time to recuperate.
2. You have given up on your quest and you are now settling for where you are.
3. You haven't seen anything else to tempt you to an even higher level of performance.

I am going to assume that point two doesn't apply to you. Point one is easy to deal with, have a time out and come back to the question later on. Point three just means that you are ready to act when you see an opportunity. Running back over the options in the first part of this book can help you to jump start this idea generation process again.

'What does good look like?' will evolve over time as your business changes. Don't forget this and re-apply the tools from this book as you see fit.

Tangible results

Please keep an eye on the tangible results that your change programme yields. There is a 'feel good' factor around making change happen to an organisation, it feels like you are making progress when things change. If, however, the changes aren't yielding any positive / tangible results for your business then simply the changes don't count. Let me give you a simple test to help you identify if your changes are tangible to the business.

If your improvement is improving the money situation of your business, then it highly likely that it has generated a tangible improvement.

For the majority of your changes the improvements you make should lead to an improvement of the money your business has to play with.

Let me give you some specifics with regards to seeing the money situation in your business change:

- If your improvement is to reduce overtime spending then your overtime bill should improve.

- If your goal is to drive up on time delivery performance your delivery adherence should be going up whilst your dedicated deliveries / air freights are reducing and you should see your sales to existing (and possibly new) customers grow, if the change is to be tangible.

- If you want to drive up your productivity then you should be able to see a cash translation of this into fewer overtime hours paid and not having to replace staff when current members leave (unless you are growing of course).

- If your inventory management processes are being improved then you should see fewer stock losses leading to lower purchasing costs and fewer delays into production, yielding less overtime and expedited shipping to your customers.

If the change doesn't link back to a financial improvement somewhere it could be argued that you haven't really made a change you have just done something that is nice.

Doing nice things isn't against the rules of course, just keep this in mind when you are justifying what you are going to be spending your time, effort and resources on. If your workplace has really low morale and needs to be sorted out, then you could argue that some 'nice' goals will be the right thing to do. However I am also pretty sure that making the place a more pleasant place to work will potentially improve a financial aspect of your business through better productivity or performance.

The point I am getting to is that you can make an improvement and watch someone else mis-manage another area of the business so that your gain is never realised. I have seen senior managers use the new found gain as a way to take their eye off the ball elsewhere – net effect is that you haven't budged an inch.

Make your improvements count and make sure, using your new and improved metrics, that they really are counting for your business.

Onwards

That's the formal part of our journey together completed. In the final chapter I shall summarise this entire book, the options that I have presented, and hopefully leave you with a few final thoughts to take away with you.

Recap

- 'Nibble' at your improvement project if you stall or lose momentum, using the Kaizen method.
- Consider the question 'how do we get our tasks back on track?' at regular intervals through the projects' life.
- Learn from your improvements using the CARL model.
- Ensure that you have regular progress review meetings for your project; plan these from the outset.
- Keep an eye out for the signs that you are winning and share these with your colleagues.
- Ensure that your improvements are becoming tangible and quantifiable. Make them really count!

The Summary

I hope that you have found this book to be useful, as you change your thinking and approach on how to define the operational excellence that you are looking for. Before I leave you, here are a few more thoughts, pointers and ideas that will keep you heading in the right direction.

A true test

Let's jump forward a short period in time. You have defined your operational vision and made it a reality and have the performance results to match...

Would others want to visit your business as an exemplar?

Does your business now exude the kinds of performance and operational systems that would make other businesses want to come and learn from you?

I am not suggesting that you consider holding tours of your business to showcase what you have built, just that it is a great yardstick for you to consider.

Will you have something worth looking at?

If you can't answer 'yes' to the questions I just posed it may be worthwhile to go back to your vision and look at it with fresh eyes and close out any gaps. If you think that the business wouldn't be worth looking at this implies that you know of a few elements that could be better. What are these and what does good look like for them?

Only the best businesses get other companies requesting to visit them and learn from them. I would love it if you became one of these businesses, but (again) I am not recommending that you take up the enquiries and start becoming a tour guide.

Would people want to visit your business if you achieved your vision?

Less formal applications

The method that I have put forward in this book might seem like an awful lot to consider. If you have some current performance challenges then I encourage you to apply the question "what does good look like?" to these specific issues in your business. By asking this question in this manner you should be able to generate some quick wins that your team can pounce on and make a difference with quickly.

Let me give you some examples:

- Visual standards – how do you want your working areas to look and be maintained?

- Meetings – how should they run, do they need fixed agendas and what do they need to produce?

- Staff behaviours – what happens when there is a clash between staff, how do you want them to work together?

- General communication – who gets to know what, when, and in what manner?

- Server storage – where do files get stored, who is responsible and what happens with stray files?

- Reports – what format, what length, what content, what actions?

- Routines – what does a brilliant day look like for your team?

- Structure of teams – how should the structure look and what skills / talents do you need within that structure?

- Standard Operating Procedures – what format should they be in, how easy should they be to use and how will they be used going forward?

- Supplier relationships – do you want partnership working with your suppliers and what interactions do you want with them?

- Accreditation processes – how do you want to manage

this through the course of a year (last minute, or cool and calm)?

This is just a broad list of areas that most businesses could consider, but hopefully one that will give you some ideas as to how you could dip your toe into the water for this approach.

If I refer back to the Kaizen approach just for a moment, you could apply this approach in a piecemeal fashion across your business. Nibbling your way through the different teams and processes may feel more comfortable for you and, if so, don't feel constrained by the process I have suggested initially. The key result is that your operational vision is created and implemented, the route you take to get there is optional.

Keep asking "what does good look like?" and keep improving the standards that you operate to.

The essence of the proposed journey

If you are feeling a little overwhelmed at what I have laid out for you in this book let me summarise the key points, to hopefully take the sting out of what you might be feeling.

In essence, the process I have proposed is:

- Generate a vision of 'what does good look like?' (either the entire business, or targeted portions).
- Consider what you need to do in order to achieve your vision.
- Pull together an action plan and execute it.

If you only improve one thing in your business, then you'll be better off than where you are today. One improvement can lead to another (and another) and before you know it you could have changed your entire organisation. I have used both approaches over the years; sometimes you need to overhaul the operations of the whole organisation. Sometimes focusing your efforts and making a few tweaks here and there will be the right approach. I will have to leave the decision with you as to which approach is required in your business. Even if you have to do something more radical and need to transform the whole operation you can do it in phases, starting with the weakest / most pressing areas first.

If you can remember the essence of my message then you will have a simple tool that you can apply widely, rapidly and effectively to change how your business performs.

If in doubt – ask 'what does good look like?' and take it from there.

What do you need to do to get started?

So, what do you need to do in order to get started?

Do you need to speak with your colleagues? Canvas opinion? Choose an area to focus on? Talk things over with your boss? Carve out some time to think?

What do you need to do in order to get this process of change started?

It is easy to read this book. It is relatively easy to think through the ideas and make some decisions about what looks good for your business. It is quite easy to look around some other organisations and get some ideas to help you develop your own plan. Planning the new habits and designing your new metrics is also on the easy side of life. Putting it into practice, now that could be a lot more interesting.

Are you ready to make some changes in your business? Are you ready to start having some confusion and some friction as you try out your new ideas? Are you prepared for some of your team not wanting to come on the journey?

Yes? Fantastic!

No? At least you're being honest I suppose. I really want you to be able to take some steps forward with this material, so here is a suggestion for you.

Look at what it is that is bothering you about the design and implementation activities of this improvement opportunity and list the items out. For each item think through what is the worst that can happen and then plan the remedy of the situation in advance. At worst you should feel better about the process of change. At best you will have a series of 'inoculations' that you can use to deal with the situations when they arise.

Do whatever you need to do to feel ready for the change. Hopefully my suggestion will get you moving in the right direction.

The changing face of 'what does good look like'

As you grow and develop as a business, what good looks like today possibly won't look as appealing as it did originally. This is a great problem to have and I have already commented on this.

I don't want your business to be the same business it used to be, I want it to be better in every way imaginable. I also want you to be able to say that you have grown and evolved as an individual.

This journey provides the opportunity to do both, so why not embrace it?

I remember thinking that my business unit (in a previous role) would be amazing if it could get its arrears to under two weeks. I got to two weeks and decided that one week would be better. We got there quickly and decided that no arrears was the thing to do; I was too influenced by the poor performance of our sister business units to think of a great vision from the outset.

At the same time one of my core machines was capable of producing twenty-five units per shift. One of the senior managers thought that thirty was the absolute maximum we could achieve on a good day. The team decided that good looked like fifty per shift, with no additional effort on the operator's part. This number would get us into a position where the customer would talk to us about additional work. We all agreed and got on with making the changes required. We flew past fifty pretty quickly and when we zipped past eighty units per shift we got the lion's share of the new work from our customer. This looked better than thirty and the machine operator wasn't working any harder!

Our productivity was pretty good at this point, but what did good look like now? We set our sights on an additional ten percent improvement, and sailed past that target. The team liked the feeling of winning and we rode the wave.

For me, my working hours were too long so I decided that I needed some more normality to my work life. I engineered a chunk of my problems out of my day and things got easier. We became the number one performing business unit (in our group) inside of six months and the teamwork was great.

The process was the same as I described before:

- We decided what good looked like.
- We figured out what we had to do to change the

situation.

- We came up with a plan and executed it.

And… we repeated this cycle.

What do you want to work on first?

Enjoy the journey

It is time for me to sign off now.

I hope that you have gained some useful ideas from this book and that you feel that you can apply the ideas to your business. The question 'what does good look like?' can be applied in so many different areas that it has turned into one of my catchphrases. The simplicity of the question makes it accessible and the accuracy of the answer makes it effective.

Whether you are planning for a full-blown overhaul of your business or just need to work with one specific individual within your business, this question should help.

I used this very question to reduce the manufacturing lead time of a business (where I was originally a struggling manager) by over 80% and improve the on-time delivery rates from around

20% to averaging over 98%. I didn't struggle day-to-day in the end!

In a different role I used the same question to reduce my working hours from in excess of seventy-five per week to just under fifty (I obviously still had a few hours to trim). I saw a better operational vision and moved towards it.

My clients have gone from being at the bottom of their supply chain league tables to the top, by asking this question. Others have resolved long running staff issues and reduced their operating costs at the same time.

Obviously, the question isn't magic. The power here is in remembering to ask the question in the first place and being able to answer it properly. This is the point of this book; asking the question enough, in all areas of your business and being able to do something meaningful with the answer.

Have fun with the question and do your best to enjoy the ride. If you generate a good answer and define a superb vision of 'good' then the destination should be worth the effort.
So, it's now time for me to stop writing and let you get on with making it happen.

I wish you all the best going forward,

Giles

Links

The following links may be useful to you as you make progress with your improvements:

Systems and Processes

To find other resources, information on my other books, toolkits and courses visit:

http://www.systemsandprocesses.co.uk/

Free OTIF report

Sign up for my regular email newsletter and get your copy of my free guide "You're Late!!!". It includes seven low cost / quick to implement strategies to help your business improve both its productivity and its delivery performance. Follow this link to get your copy:

http://www.systemsandprocesses.co.uk/free-on-time-delivery-improvement-guide/

Blog

News, ideas and improvement methods are all shared on my blog. You can read it at:

http://www.systemsandprocesses.co.uk/blog/

Twitter

For those of you who embrace social media, you can get my tweets by following me using the handle @betterfasternow.

https://twitter.com/betterfasternow

About Giles

Giles is a Chartered Engineer with a background in Production Engineering and Operations Management. He spends most of his time working on Lean, ERP and Operations Management improvement projects.

Giles has worked in a variety of different roles within manufacturing prior to working as a consultant for a prestigious university.

In 2005 Giles decided to forge his own path and created Smartspeed, which has been helping businesses to improve their delivery performance and productivity levels, along with their profits, ever since.

Giles can be contacted by:

Email -   gilesjohnston@smartspeed.co.uk

Website -   www.smartspeed.co.uk

Printed in Great Britain
by Amazon

73956065R00099